Exeter Maps

Exeter Maps

Todd Gray

THE
MINT
PRESS

First published in Great Britain by The Mint Press, 2006

ISBN 1-903356-48-2

Cataloguing in Publication Data
CIP record for this title is available from the British Library

The Mint Press
76 Longbrook Street
Exeter, Devon
England EX4 6AP

Typeset by Kestrel Data
Cover design by Delphine Jones

Printed and bound in Great Britain
by Short Run Press Ltd, Exeter

Introduction

Exeter has an impressive number of maps of great quality and distinction. The great Elizabethan map by John Hooker has been pre-eminent for hundreds of years. It influenced several generations of map-makers and continues to fascinate Exeter people and all those interested in maps. There are however dozens of other maps which are also of great interest.

This booklet shows some of them and is intended to indicate how rich Exeter's map history is. It cannot claim to be comprehensive in any way: it is merely a selection of some of the printed ones which have been produced over the last five centuries. There are also many manuscript maps.

The city has benefited from the expertise of Professor W. L. D. Ravenhill, Margery Rowe, Mary Ravenhill and Ian Maxted in interpreting many of these maps and hopefully some day we will have a definite work on the several hundred maps which can tell us so much about Exeter and the history of map-making. Until then, this booklet indicates some of Exeter's map treasures.

The maps in this book comprise:

1587 — Exeter's most famous map. John Hooker, the city's Chamberlain, first historian and archivist, was responsible for this iconic view of Exeter – a 'bird's eye view as it would appear from the western suburb of St Thomas. The four main gates are shown (North leading out towards the parish of St David, East to Sidwell Street, South on the road to the parish of St Leonard and West towards Exe Bridge) as well as Water Gate at the Quay. Hooker's map was printed by Franciscus Hogenberg.

There are three surviving 'states' or versions of the map. Each has minor differences. The most noticeable occur at the bottom right. The British Library state has a pair of dividers whereas of the two owned by Exeter City Council one has a compass rose and on the other it has been erased and the line of the road towards St Leonard's parish has been moved. There are other subtle differences.

1618 — Hooker's map formed the basis for Exeter's later maps for several generations. This map was engraved by Braun & Hogenberg and published in Cologne. This version was reprinted in 1800. Exeter continues to be represented as a tightly-built walled city with a nearly circular shape.

1677 — A map printed for one of John Hooker's successors, Richard Izacke, who also copied much of Hooker's written works on Exeter. This appeared in Izacke's *Antiquities of the City of Exeter* and was influenced by Hooker and John Speed's map of 1611. New details are included including place names.

1709 — This map originated by an individual with the most unusual name amongst the surveyors, Ichabod Fairlove. It was engraved by Joseph Coles and dedicated to local surgeon Caleb Lowdham. This was a new survey of the city. The map has unusual vignettes of Exeter buildings, notably two new stunning city buildings (the workhouse on Heavitree Road and the Customs House at the Quay) as well as the front of the Guildhall and the Cathedral. The cloth racks are distinctly shown but have disappeared from Friernhay, the city's graveyard since 1637. The embellishments to Fairlove's map appear to the right.

1723 — A reworking of Fairlove's map by John Stukeley with none of his outer embellishments. Nevertheless there are subtle additions. The cloth trade was at its height at this time and had created great wealth in the city and within its vast hinterland.

1744–64 — This was a milestone in Exeter mapping in 1744. John Rocque was a Huguenot who worked in many other parts of England and his map has extraordinary vignettes which were not included in this compressed version in 1764. The early eighteenth-century growth of Exeter can be clearly seen in the parishes of St David and St Sidwell. Paris Street is noted as Paree Street and Southernhay was then being developed including the recent building of Dean Clarke's new hospital. The City Hospital, near where the city's coach station currently is located, and the Workhouse (later City Hospital) are also marked.

1765 — Benjamin Donn, born in Bideford, produced his 'plan of the city and suburbs of Exeter' as part of his extensive work on Devon not long after Rocque's map was printed. There are subtle differences between them. His work on the county is perhaps better known and regarded but his Exeter map is still remarkable.

1792 — This is perhaps a more artistic map of the city which was surveyed by Charles Tozer. New building developments can be seen such as part of Bedford Circus and the disappearance of ancient landmarks including the Great Conduit from the Carfax (the corner of North, South, Fore and High Streets) and of East and North Gates. At the figure's feet lies a copy of Izacke's work on Exeter.

1805 — John Hayman drew this map comparatively recently after Tozer's work was published. It formed part of *The Beauties of England and Wales* by J. Britton and E. W. Brayley.

1835 — Twenty years later R. Brown created yet another map. The growth of the suburbs of the city can perhaps be most easily discerned but there are many other developments depicted including the creation of the Basin by the quay, the carving out of Queen Street, the building of the city prison (where the Rougemont Hotel now stands), the completion of Bedford Circus and the removal of the remaining City Gates. It was made shortly after the outbreak of cholera in 1832 and hints at the great changes then being made to Exeter in an attempt to prevent further outbreaks of disease.

1850 — John Warren's map continues to show change: the railway arrived only six years earlier and the line is marked along the river. Large homes are seen in the suburbs and the two new markets have been built in Fore and Queen Streets. The rate of change had accelerated.

1852 — The map by J. Rapkin for John Tallis was published only two years later and is a much more simpler and elegant. Many of the details are nevertheless different.

1881 — Henry Besley's *Exeter Directory* was an influential means by which local people received maps and this map was one of those printed by him. It shows the creation of Newtown then taking place and many other streets being carved out of local fields such as Prospect Park.

1888 — Ordnance Survey maps had been known for several generations when this map of six inches to one statute mile was published. It was reprinted in 1899 and provides a way of representing Exeter which continues today.

1890 — This map, of 25.344 inches to a statute mile was reprinted in 1903. The details of local streets and buildings are compelling.

1910 — Henry Besley impressive view of Exeter from St Thomas almost harks back to Hooker's map of 1587. This map shows a city with constant and incremental growth and change but untouched by war since the 1640s and the sieges by the Royalists and Parliamentarians.

1941 — A German map of the city potentially useful for bombing or for an invasion. It is not known if the map was used during the Blitz in May 1942 when much of the centre was devastated by an unimaginable level of destruction.

Copyright for all these printed maps rests with the Westcountry Studies Library, part of Devon County Council, to which I am grateful for permission to publish them.

The S.º West Prospect of the Cathedral.

The Guild-Hall.

The Work=house

The Custom=house

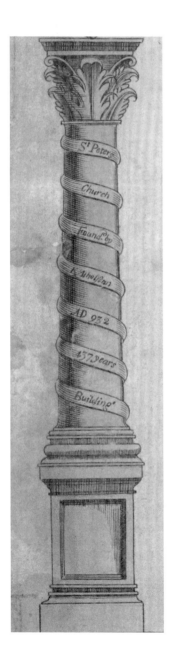

For Ian Maxted, whose work runs through the history of maps in Exeter and in many
other Devon topics written by a generation of librarians, historians and archivists

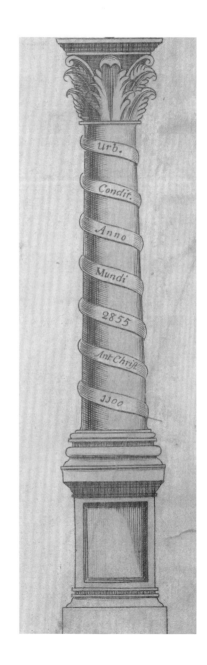

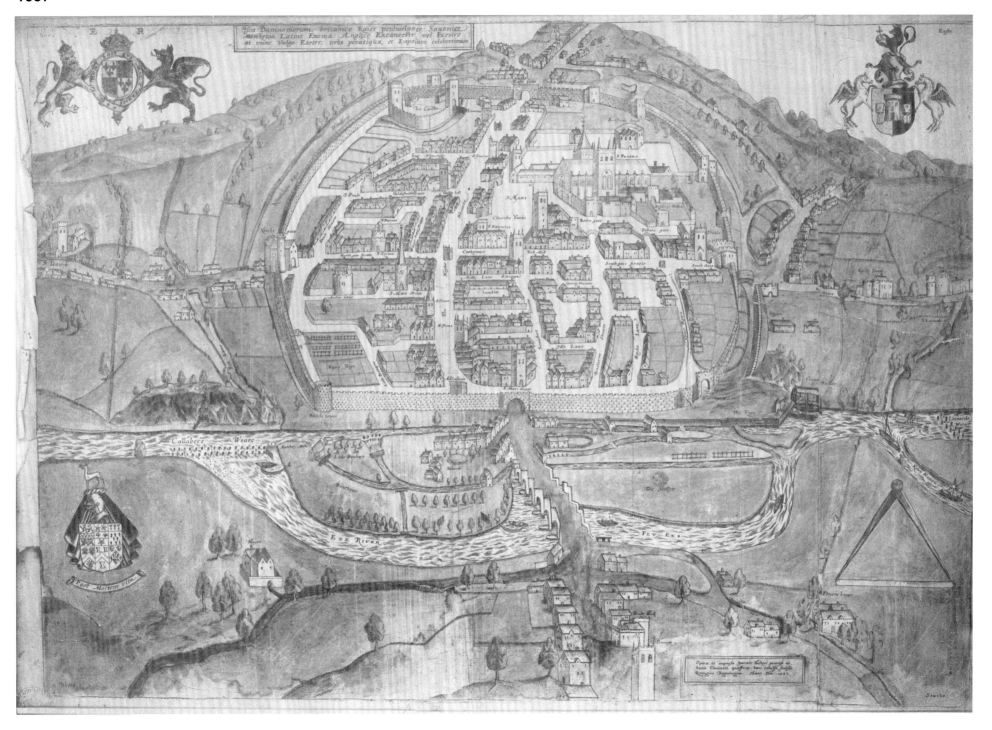

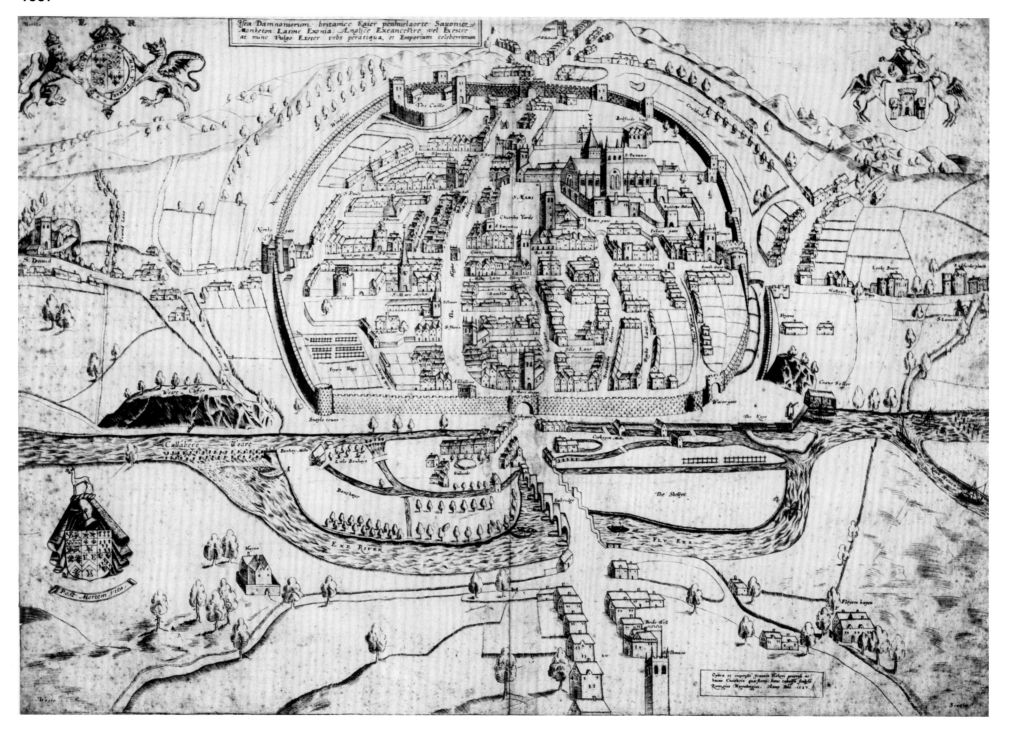

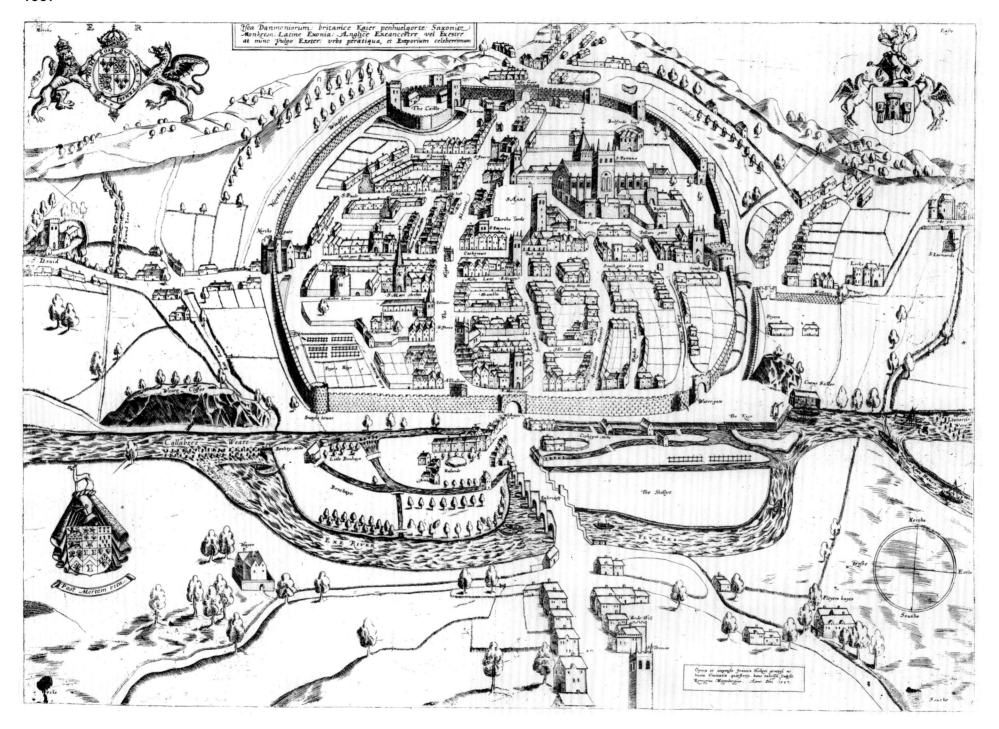

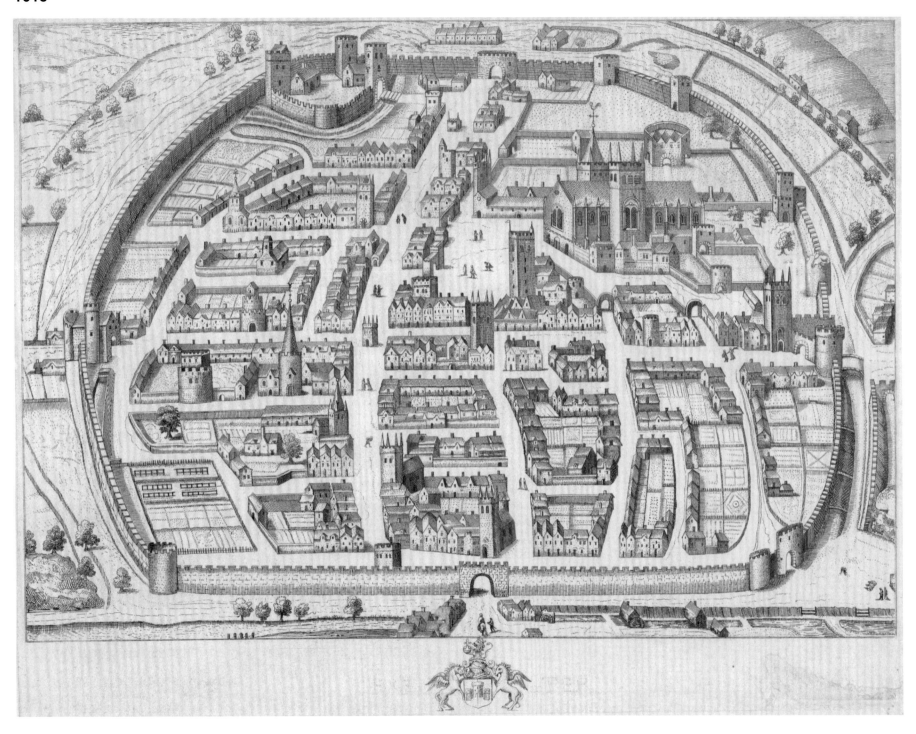

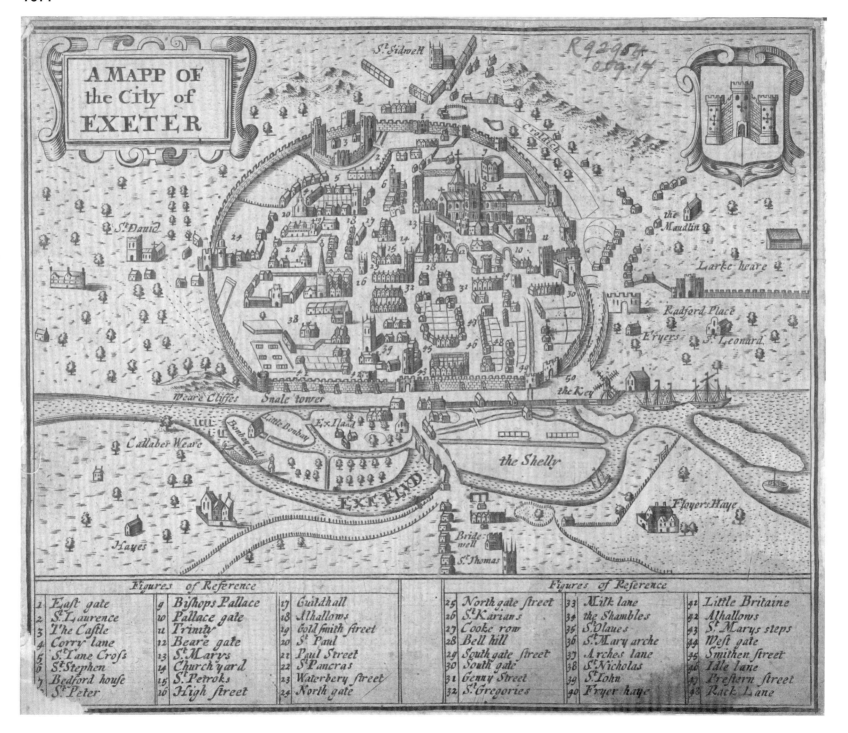

A MAPP OF the City of EXETER

Figures of Reference

1 East gate	9 Bishops Pallace	17 Guildhall	25 North gate street	33 Milk lane	41 Little Britaine
2 St Laurence	10 Pallace gate	18 Alhallows	26 St Karians	34 the Shambles	42 Alhallows
3 The Castle	11 Trinity	19 Goldsmith street	27 Cooke row	35 St Olaues	43 St Marys steps
4 Corry lane	12 Beare gate	20 St Paul	28 Bell hill	36 St Mary arche	44 West gate
5 St Iane Cross	13 St Marys	21 Paul Street	29 South gate street	37 Arches lane	45 Smithen street
6 St Stephen	14 Church yard	22 St Pancras	30 South gate	38 St Nicholas	46 Idle lane
7 Bedford house	15 St Petroks	23 Waterbery street	31 Genny Street	39 St Iohn	47 Prestern street
8 St Peter	16 High street	24 North gate	32 St Gregories	40 Fryer haye	48 Rack Lane

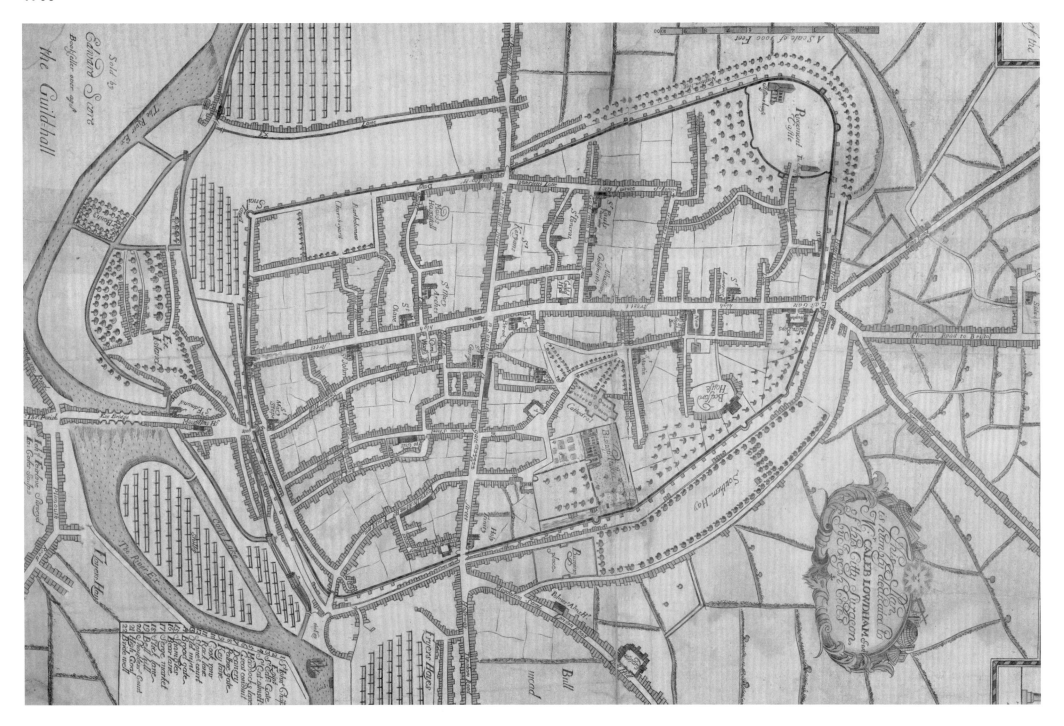

1723

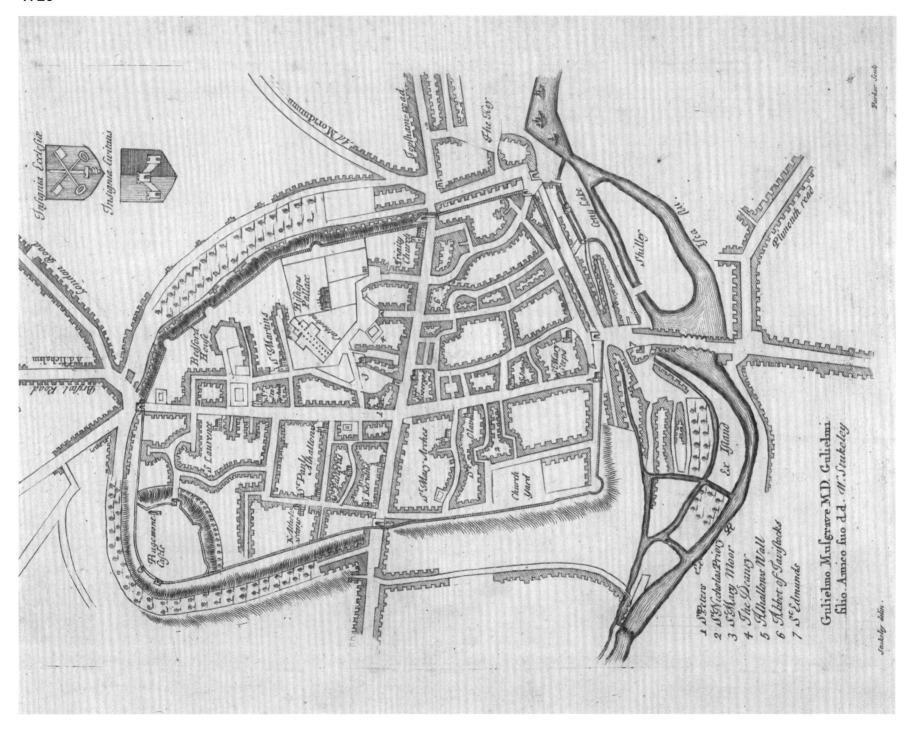

15

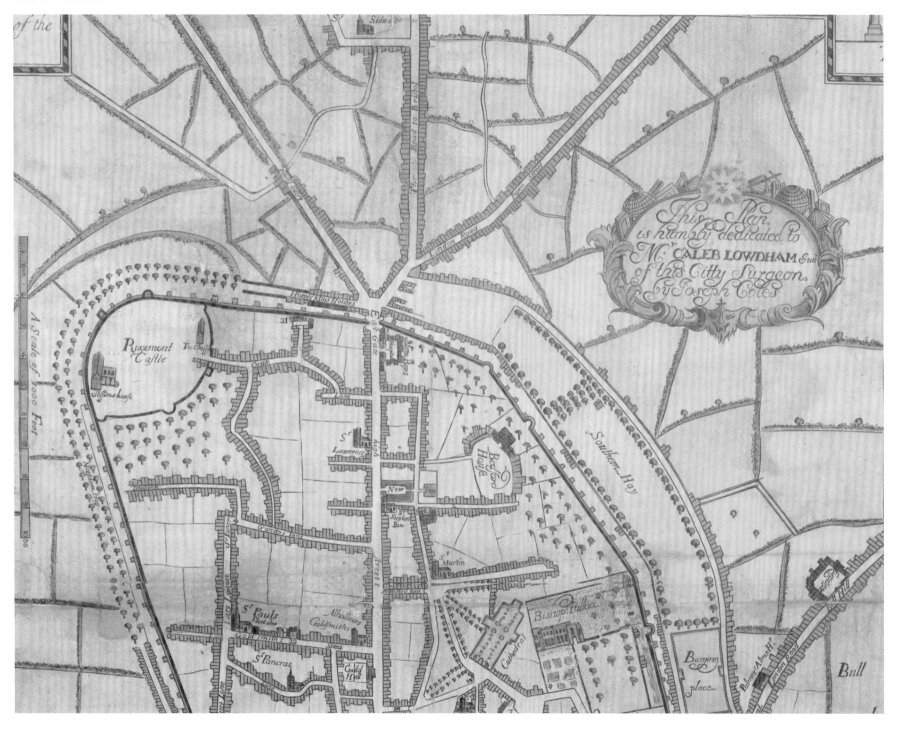

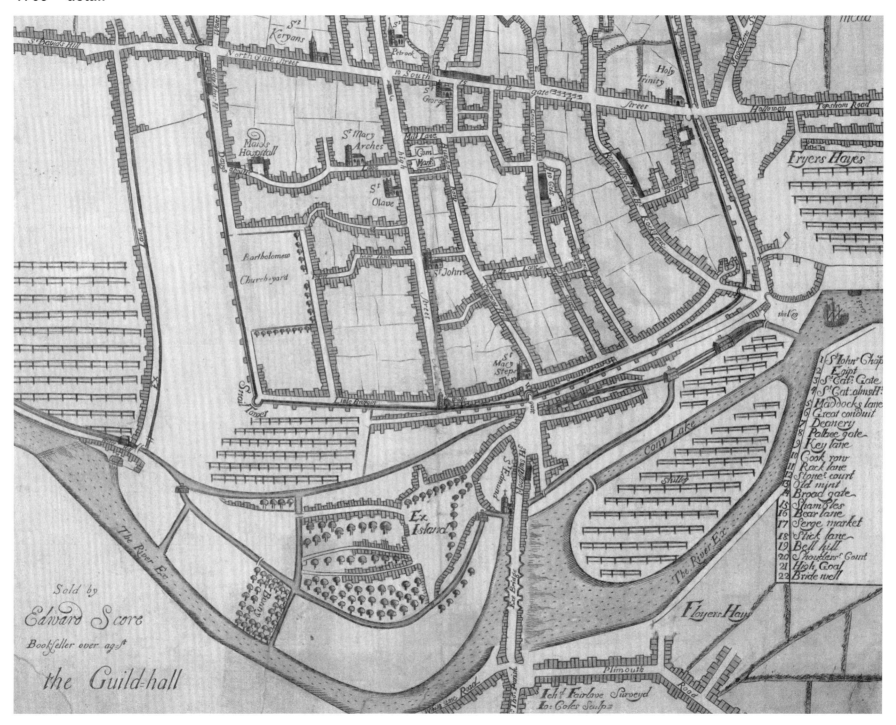

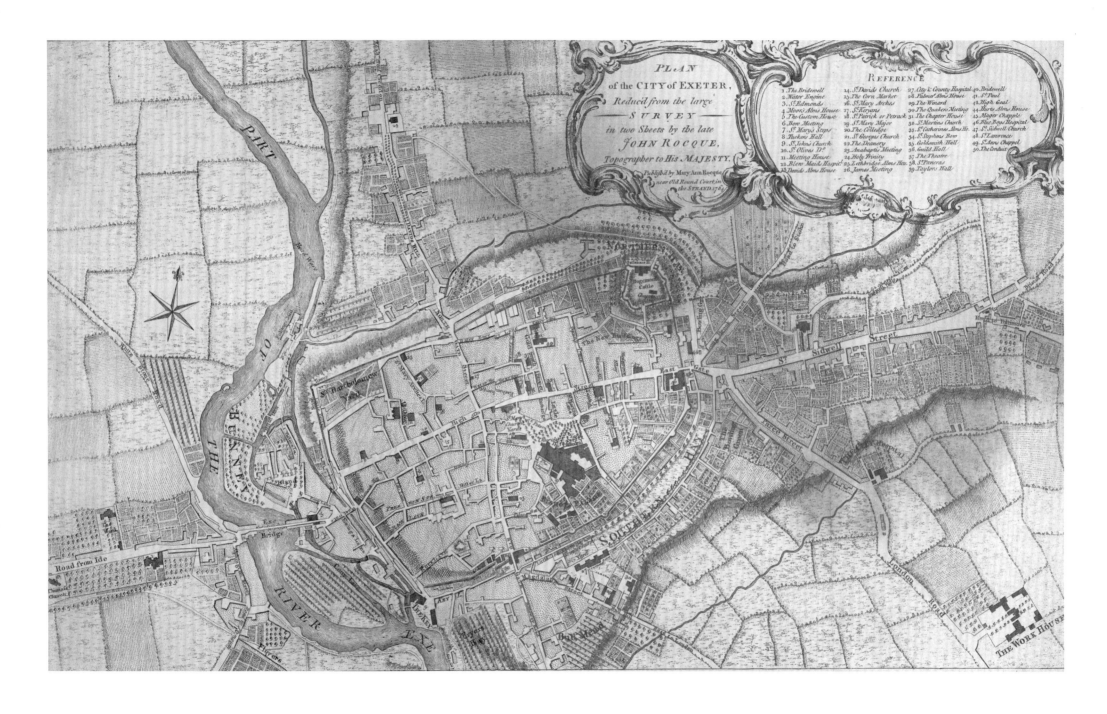

PLAN of the CITY of EXETER, Reduced from the large SURVEY in two Sheets by the late JOHN ROCQUE, Topographer to His MAJESTY.

Publish'd by Mary Ann Rocque, near Old Round Court, in the STRAND. 1764

REFERENCE

1. The Bridewell
2. Water Engine
3. St. Edmonds
4. Moors Alms House
5. The Custom House
6. Bow Meeting
7. St. Marys Steps
8. Tuckers Hall
9. St. Johns Church
10. St. Olives Do.
11. Meeting House
12. Blew Maid Hospit.
13. Davids Alms House
14. St. Davids Church
15. The Corn Market
16. St. Mary Arches
17. St. Kerians
18. St. Patrick or Petrock
19. St. Mary Major
20. The Colledge
21. St. Georges Church
22. The Deanery
23. Anabaptis Meeting
24. Holy Trinity
25. Lethbridge Alms Hou.
26. James Meeting
27. City & County Hospital
28. Palmers Alms House
29. The Winard
30. The Quakers Meeting
31. The Chapter House
32. St. Martins Church
33. St. Catharines Alms Ho.
34. St. Stephens Bow
35. Goldsmith Hall
36. Guild Hall
37. The Theatre
38. St. Pancras
39. Taylors Hall
40. Bridewell
41. St. Paul
42. High Goal
43. Thirts Alms House
44. Magor Chapple
45. Blue Boys Hospital
46. St. Sidwell Church
47. St. Lawrence
48. St. Anns Chapel
49. The Conduit

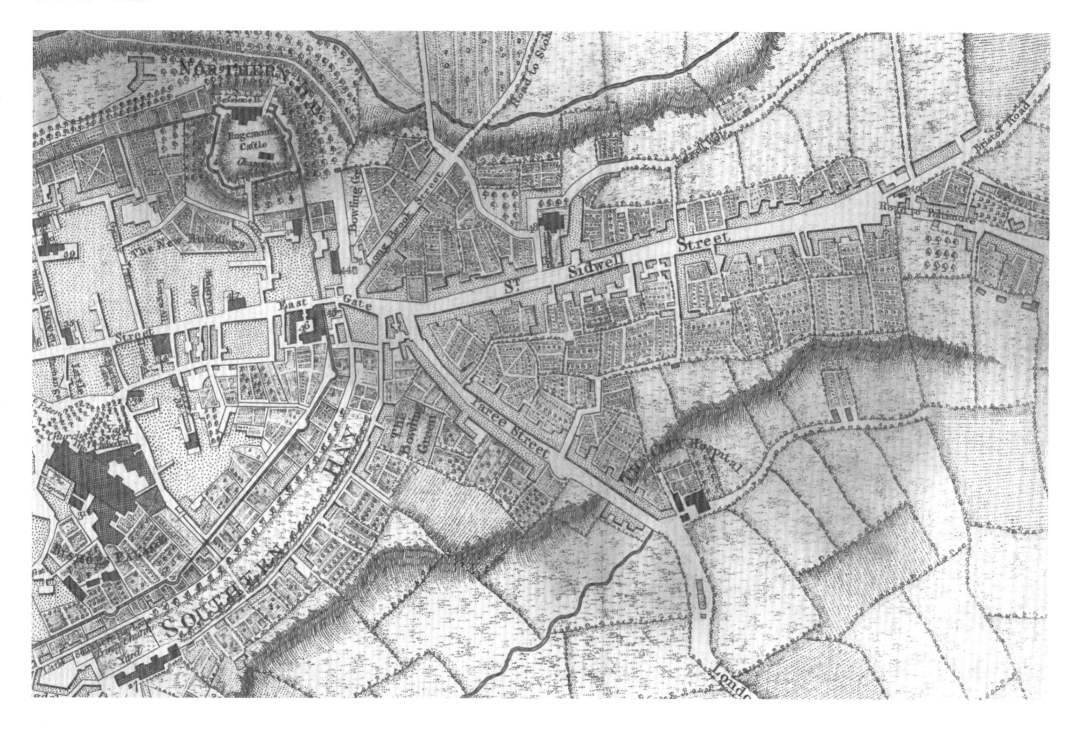

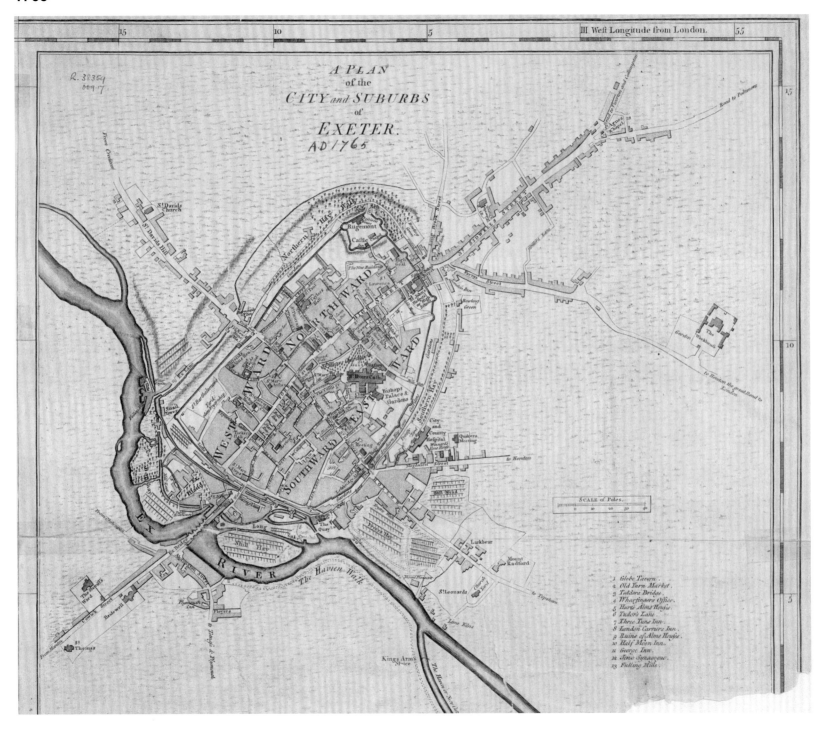

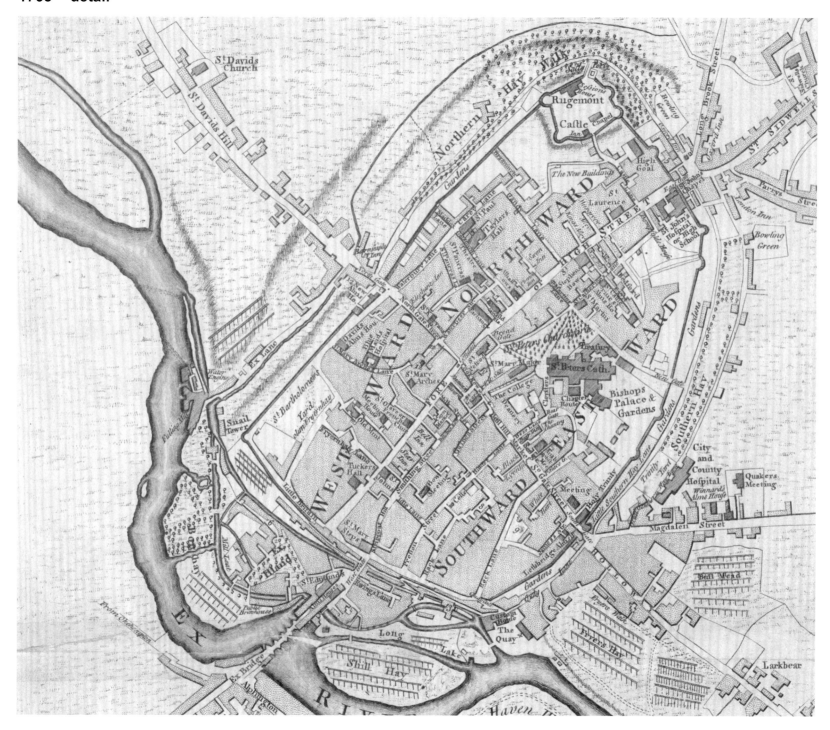

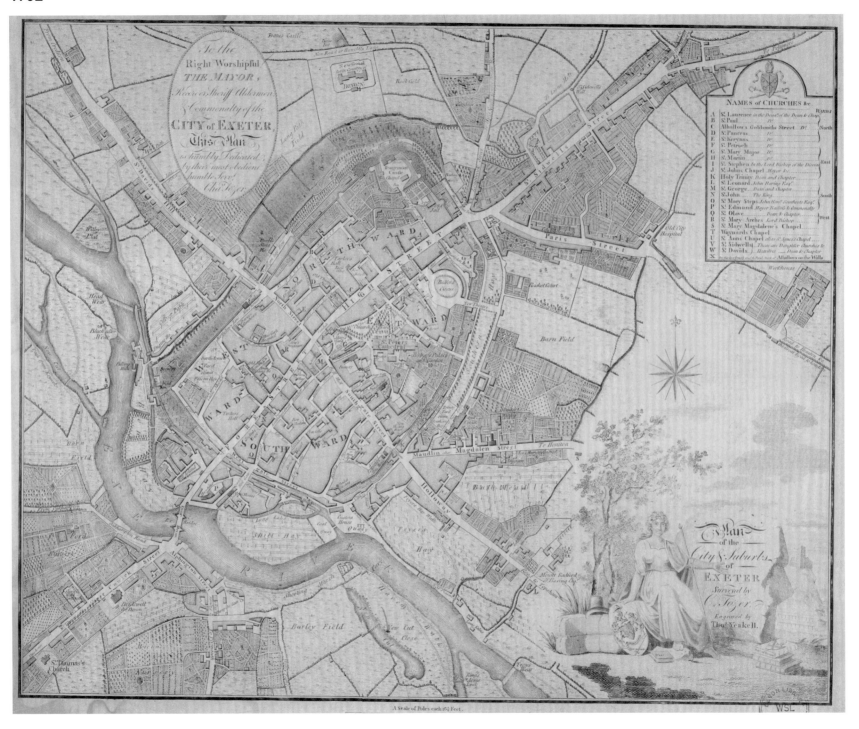

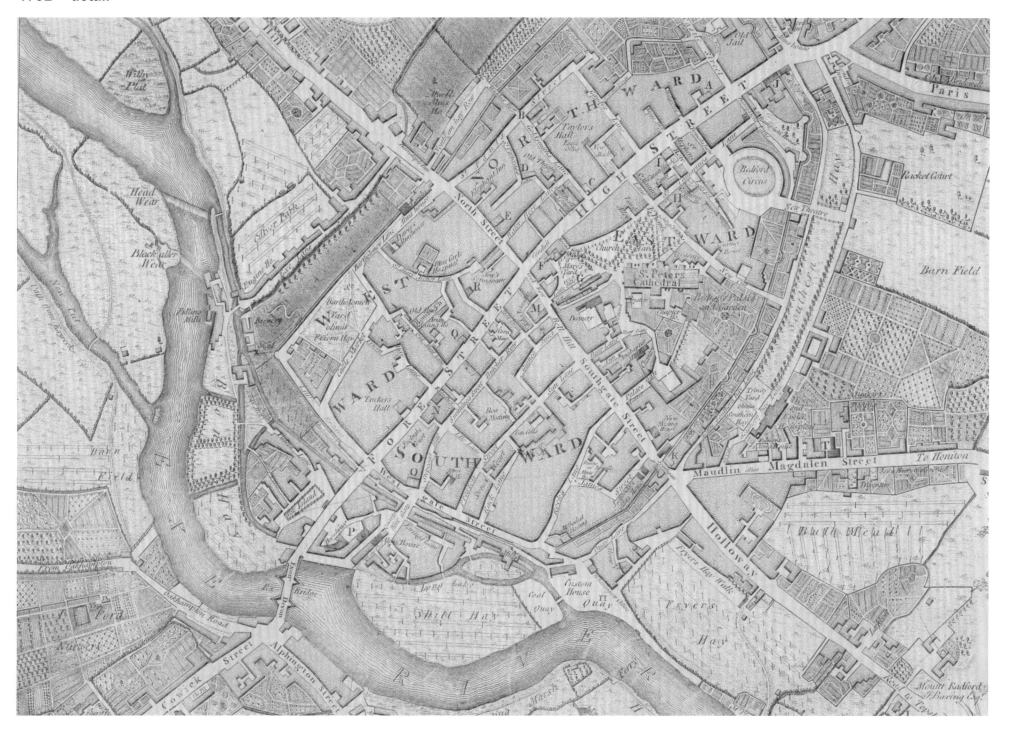

EXETER

By J.Roper from a Drawing by T.Hayman.

London: Published for the Proprietors by Vernor & Hood Poultry, June 1st 1805.

Drawn and Engraved under the direction of J. Britton.

to accompany the Beauties of England and Wales.

RIVER EXE

ST THOMAS STREET

FORE STREET

HIGH STREET

MAGDALEN STREET

SOUTH STREET

PARIS STREET

ST SIDWELL STREET

LONGBROOK STREET

BARRACKS

Rougemont Castle

New Canal

Path to Exwick

SCALE

REFERENCE.

E East Ward
1 St Peters Cathedral & Chu Yard
2 St Mary Majors Ch & Ch Yard
3 St Petrocks Church
4 St Pancras Church
5 St Martins Church
6 St Stephens Church
7 Mayors Chapel & Blue School
8 Quakers Meeting House
9 Holy Trinity Church
10 Anabaptists Meeting House

N North Ward
11 Methodists Meeting House
12 St Lawrence's Church
13 St Pauls Church
14 Allhallows Church
15 St Kerrians Church
16 St Pancras Church
17 St Davids Church
18 St Edwells Church

W West Ward
19 St Mary Arches Church
20 Jews Synagogue
21 St Olaves Church
22 Arians Meeting House
23 Roman Catholic Meet g House
24 Allhallows on the Water

S South Ward
25 St Georges Ch & Great Conduit
26 St Johns Church
27 St Mary Steps Church
28 Bow Dissenters Meeting House
29 St Edmunds Church
30 Methodists Meeting House
31 St Leonards Chapel

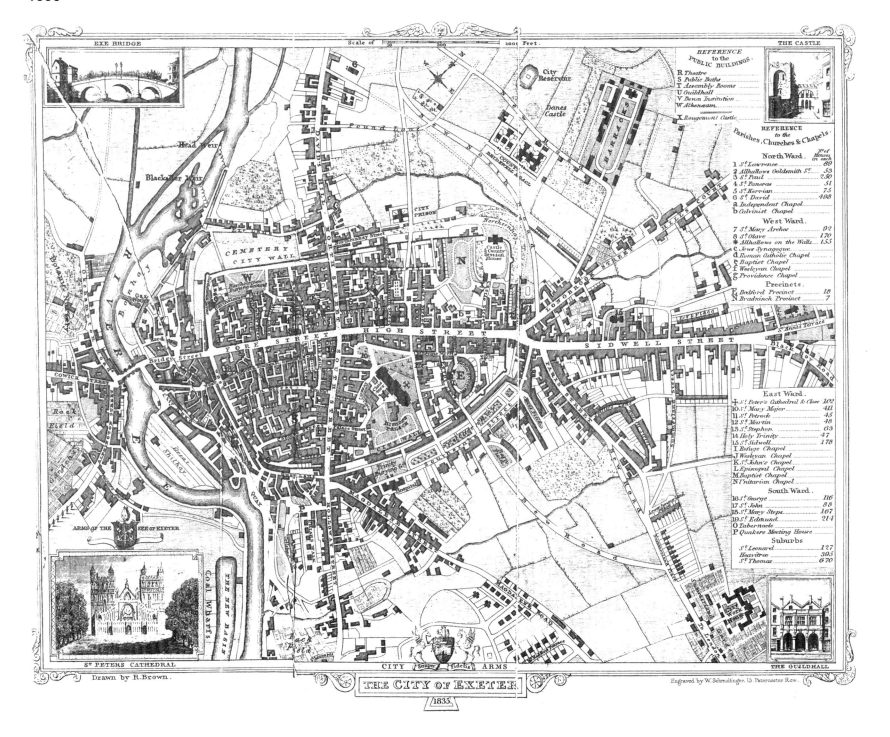

THE CITY OF EXETER

1835

Drawn by R.Brown.

Engraved by W.Schmollinger, 13 Paternoster Row.

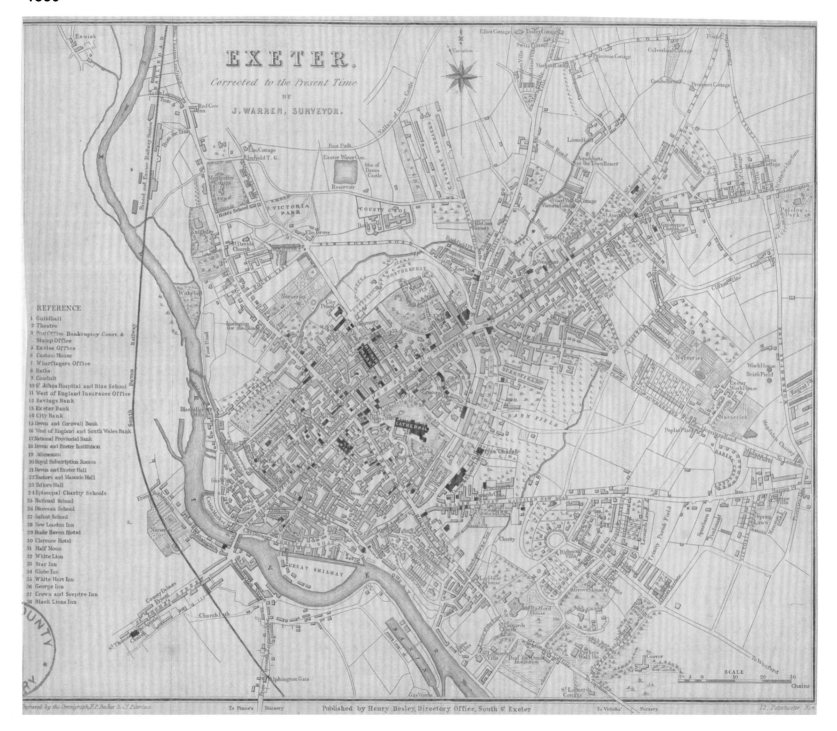

REFERENCE
1 Guildhall
2 Theatre
3 Post Office Bankruptcy Court &
   Stamp Office
4 Excise Office
5 Custom House
6 Wharfingers Office
7 Baths
8 Conduit
9 St. Johns Hospital and Blue School
10 West of England Insurance Office
11 Savings Bank
12 Exeter Bank
13 City Bank
14 Devon and Cornwall Bank
15 West of England and South Wales Bank
16 National Provincial Bank
17 Devon and Exeter Institution
18 Athenæum
19 Royal Subscription Rooms
20 Devon and Exeter Hall
21 Backers and Masonic Hall
22 Tailors Hall
23 Episcopal Charity Schools
24 National School
25 Diocesan School
26 Infant School
27 New London Inn
28 Bude Haven Hotel
29 Clarence Hotel
30 Half Moon
31 White Lion
32 Star Inn
33 Globe Inn
34 White Hart Inn
35 George Inn
36 Crown and Sceptre Inn
37 Black Lions Inn

EXETER,
Corrected to the Present Time
BY
J. WARREN, SURVEYOR.

1852

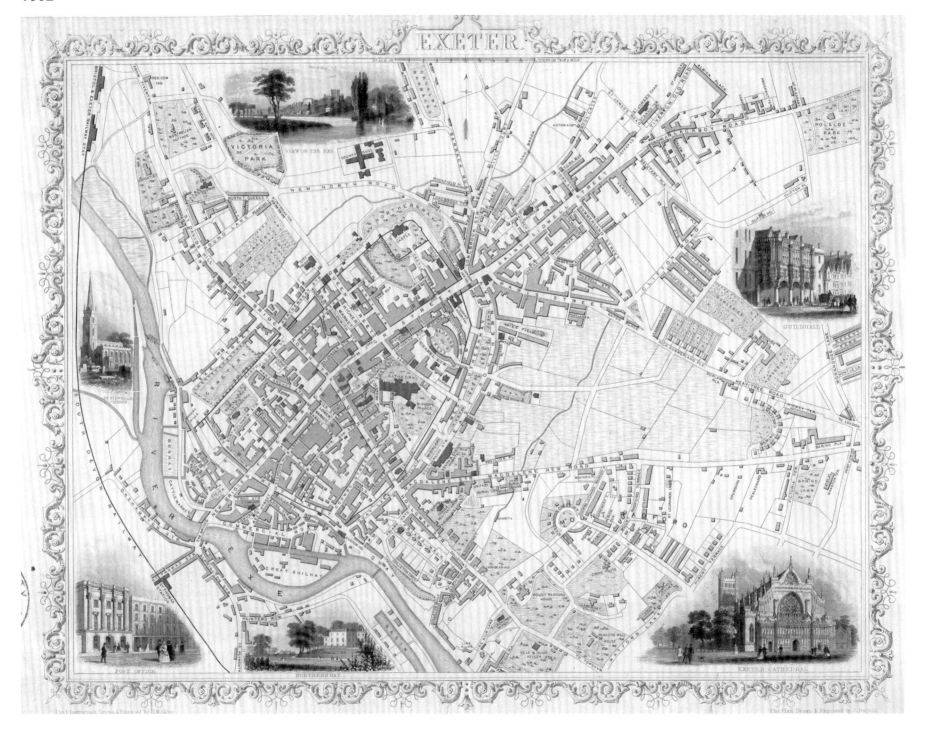

27

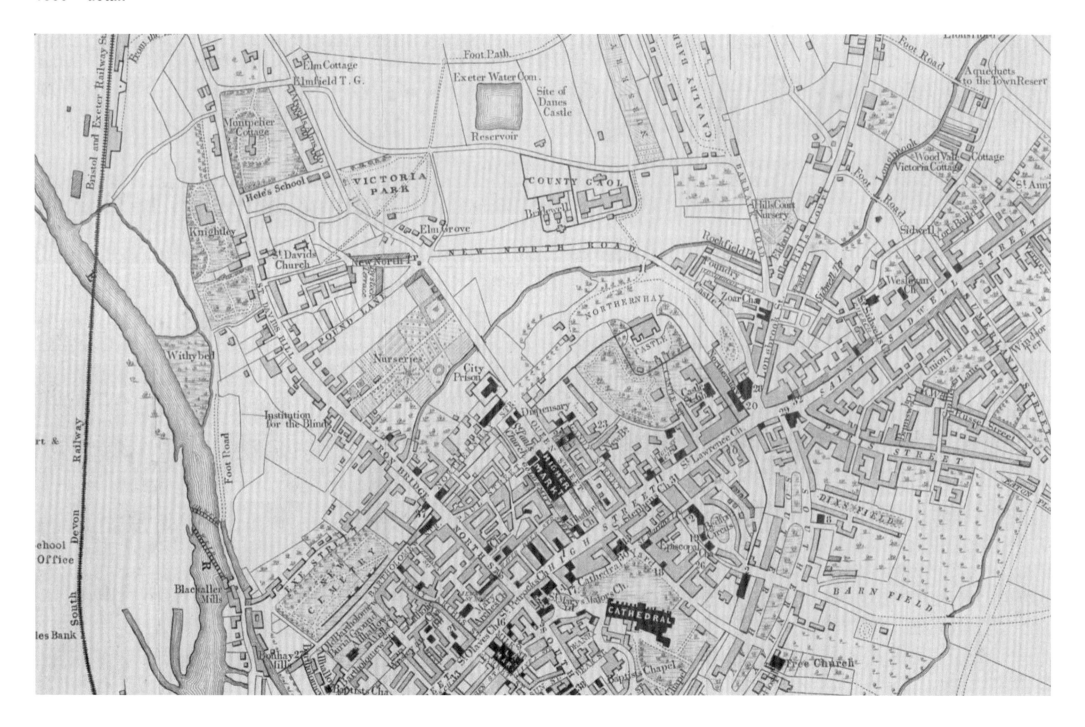

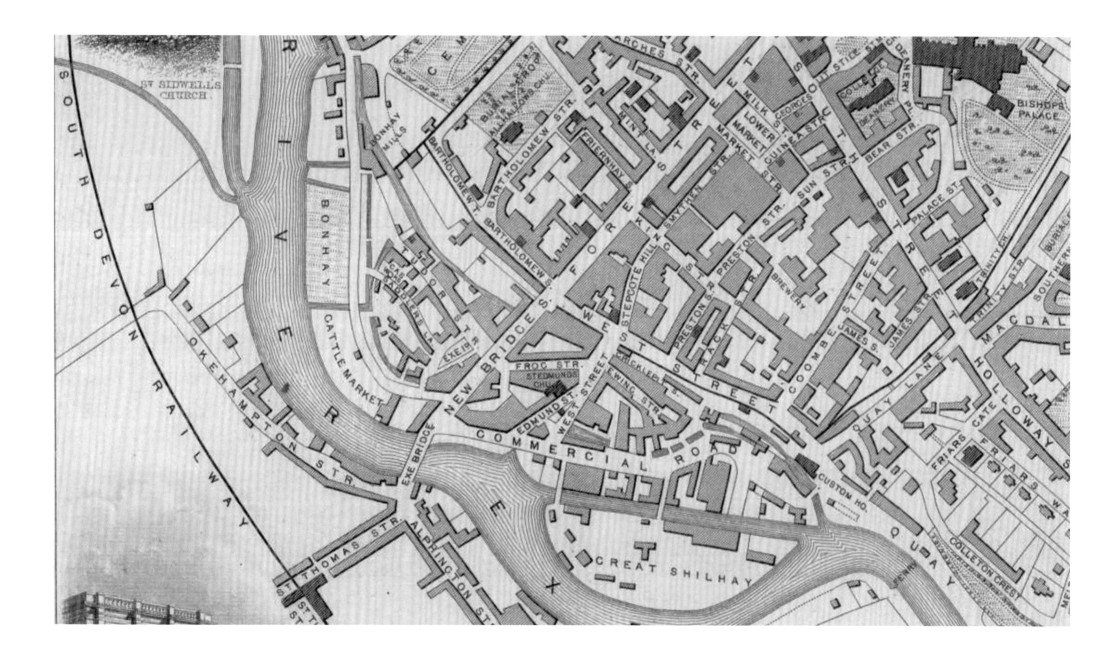

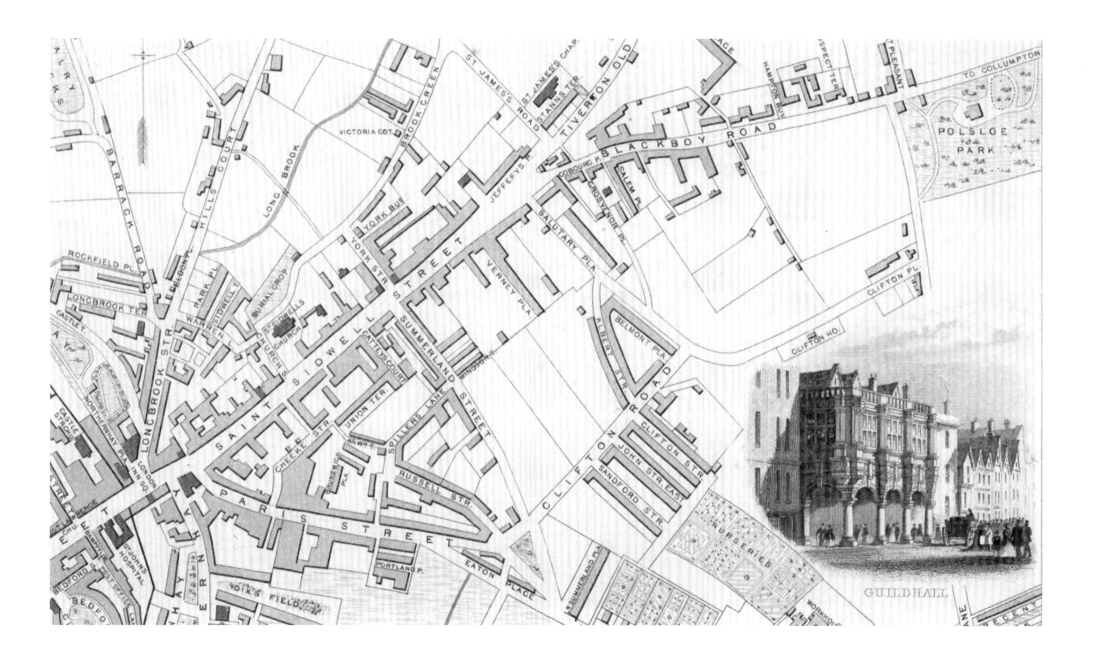

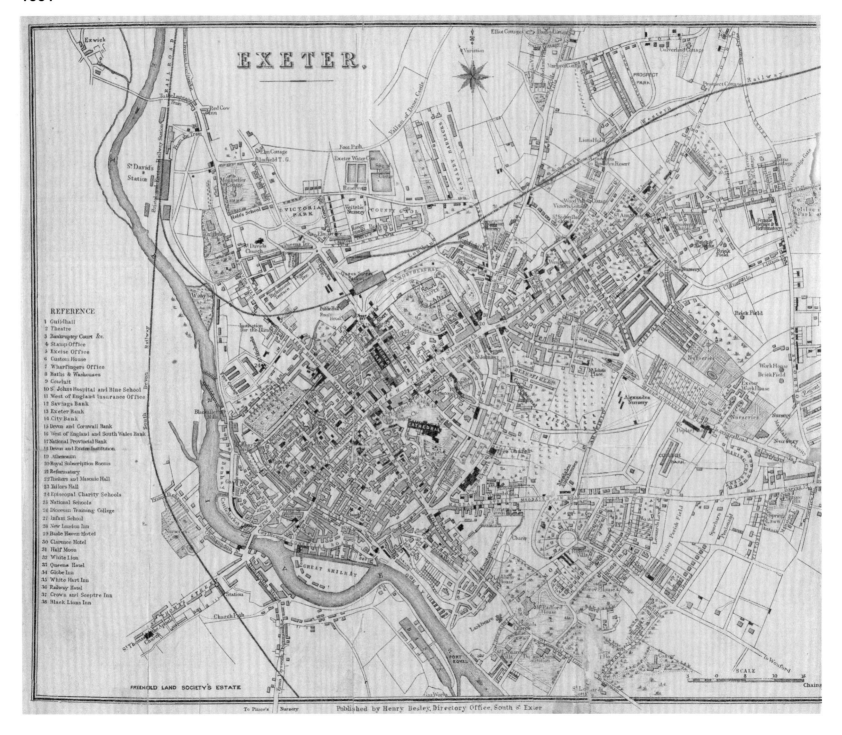

EXETER.

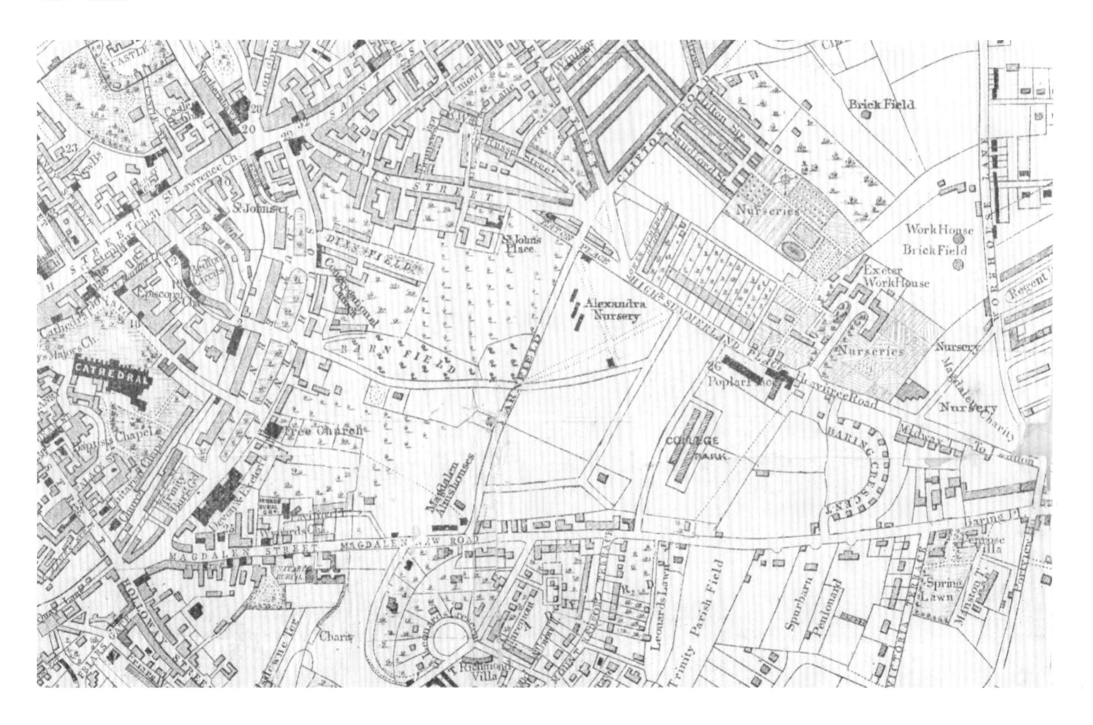

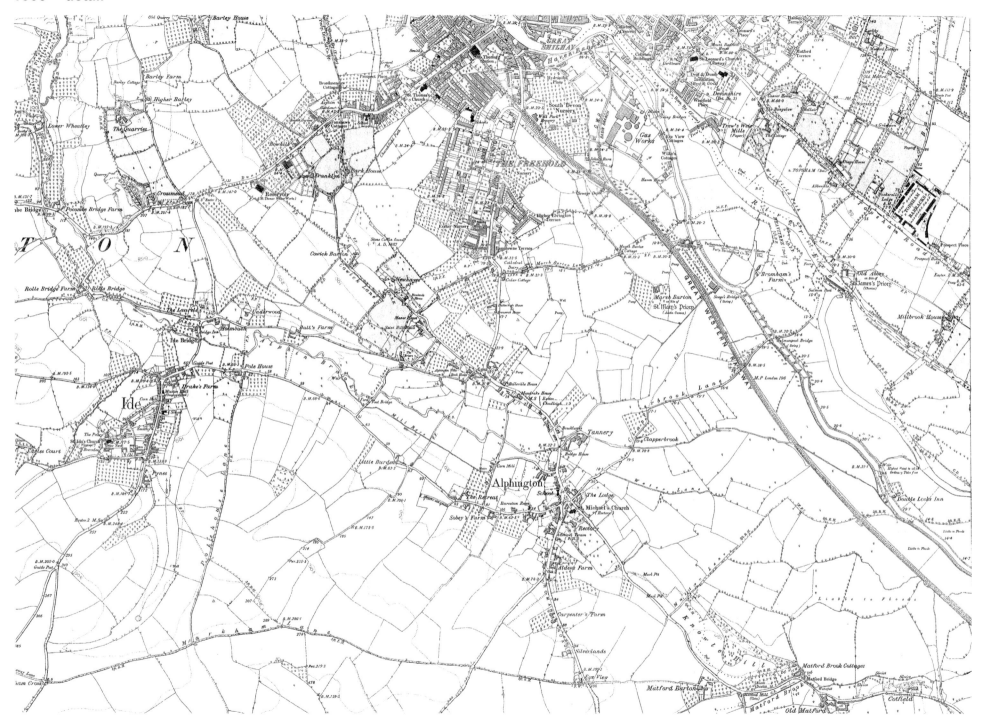

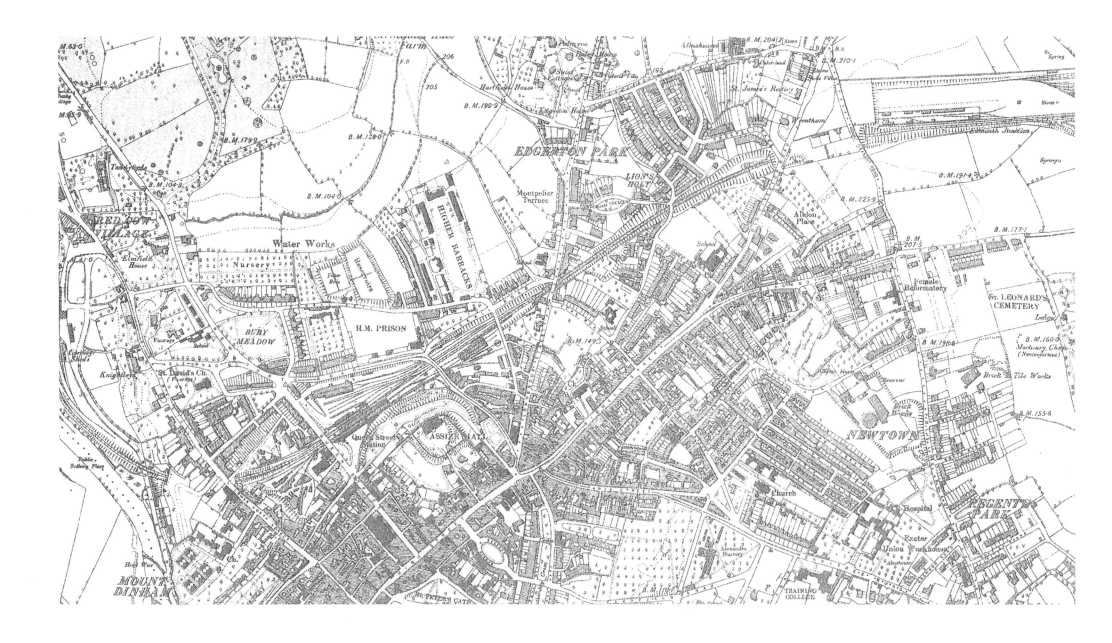

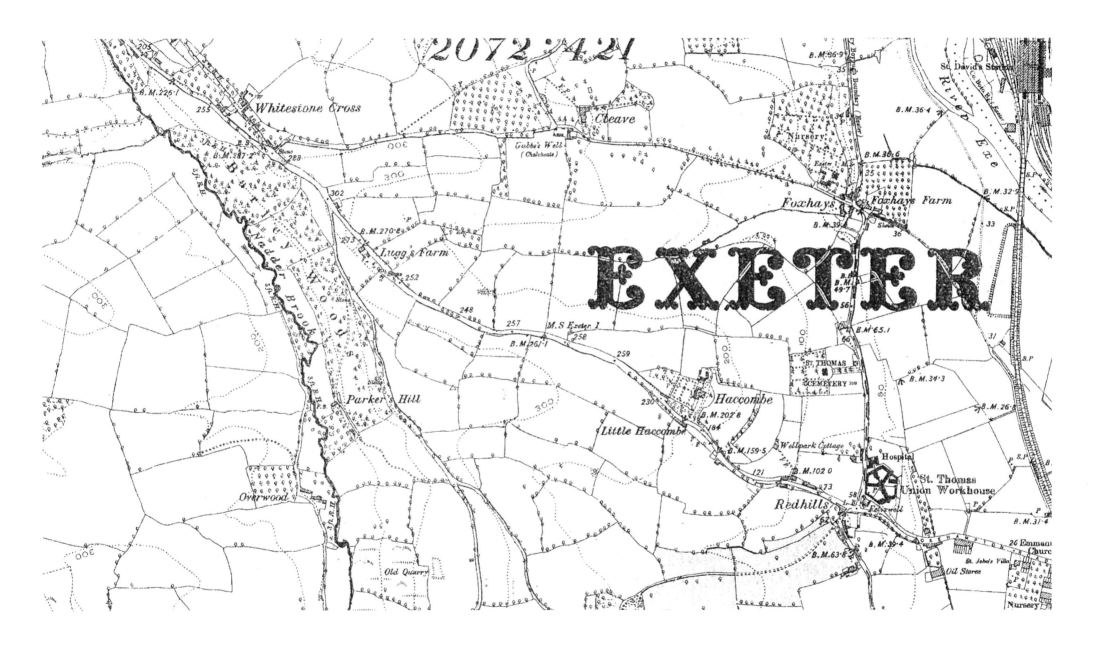

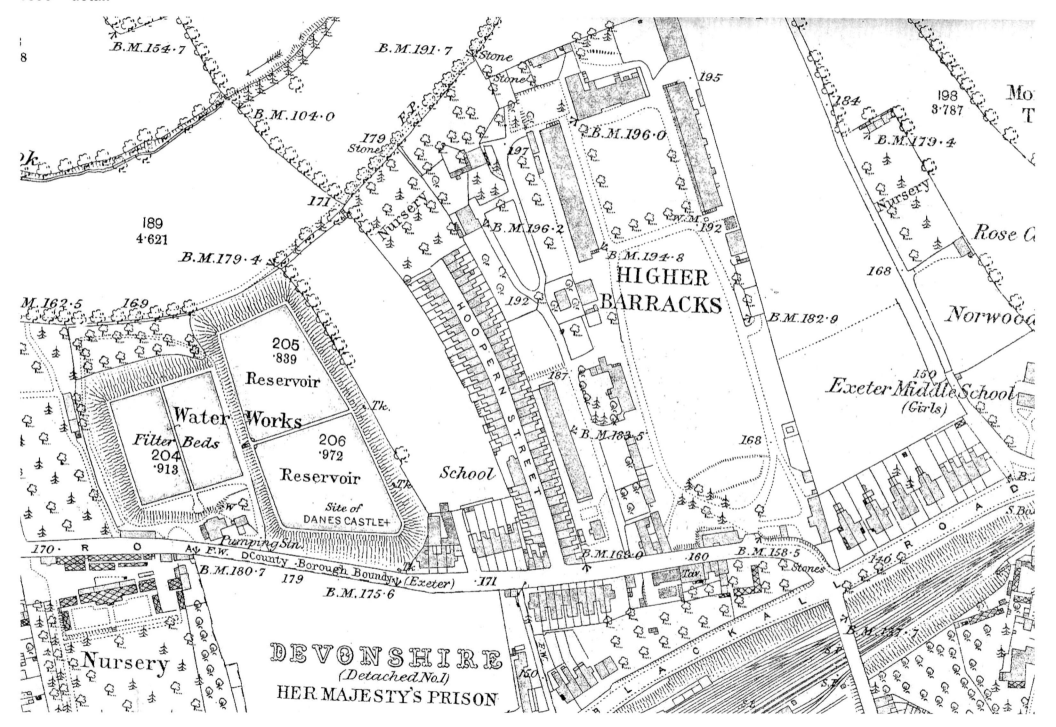

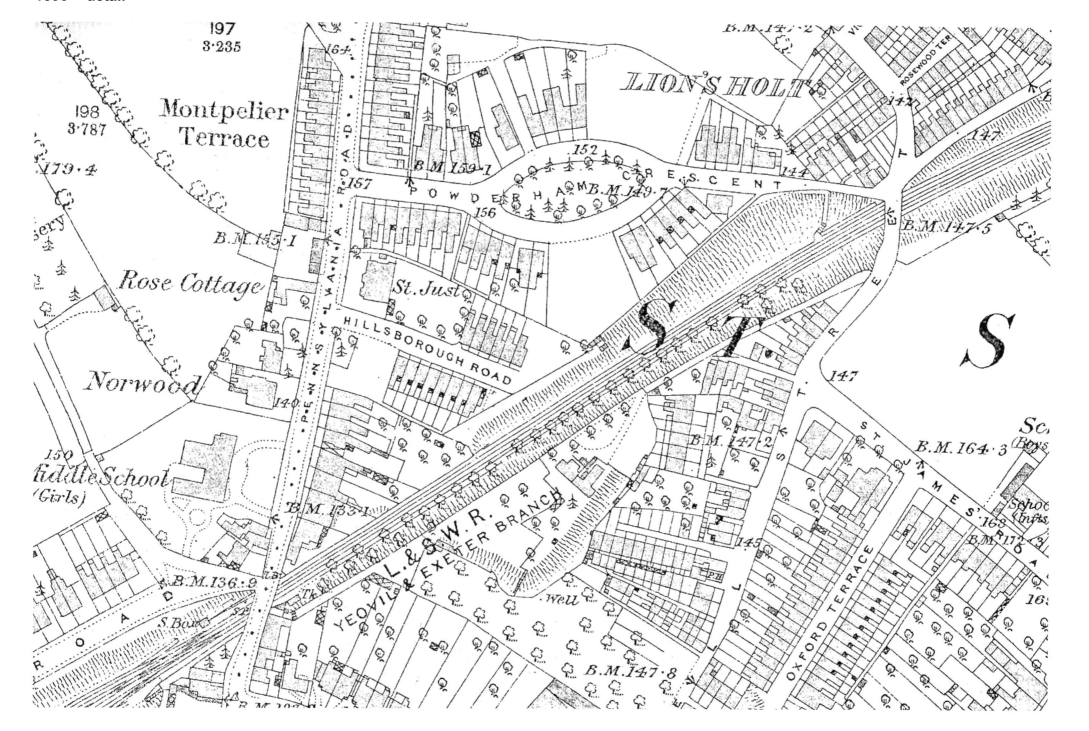

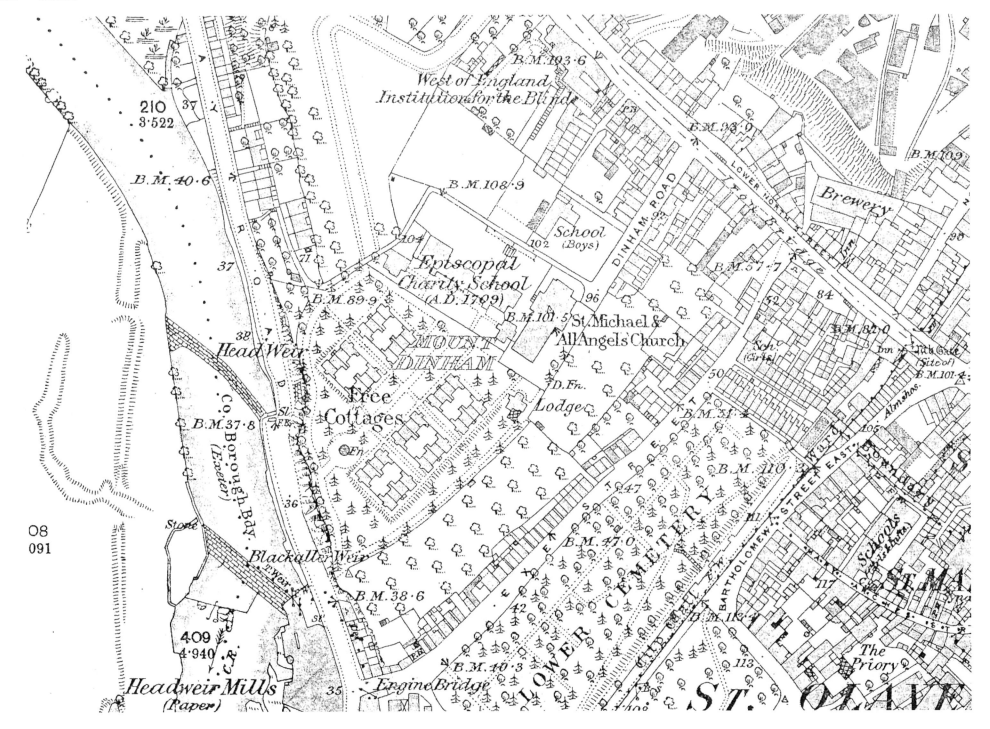

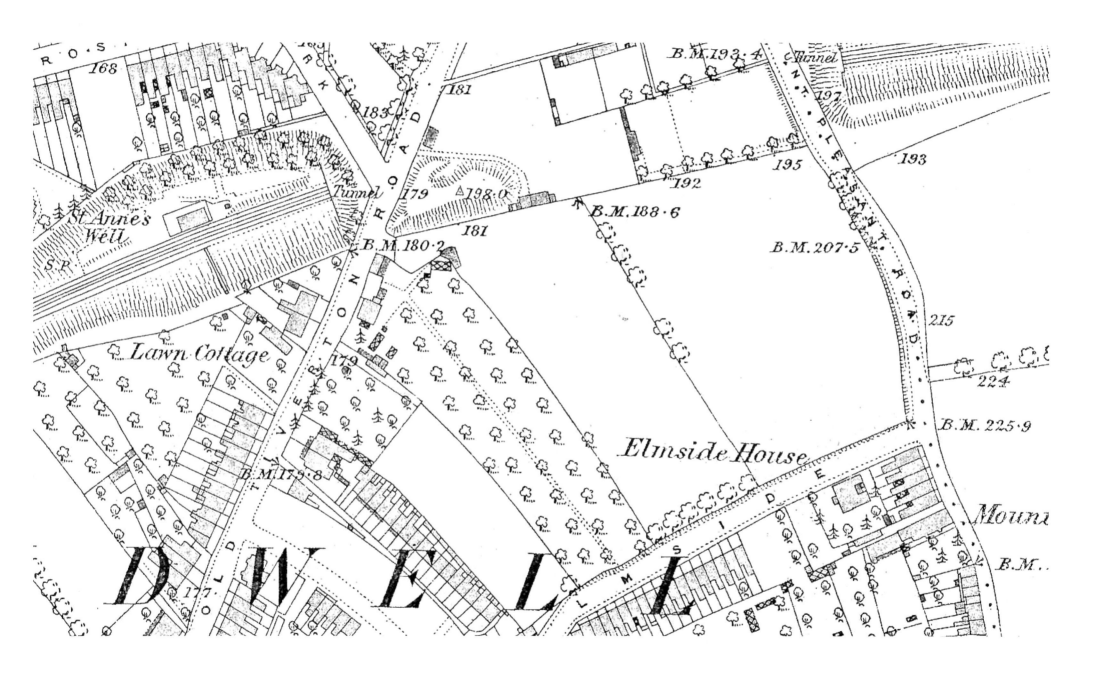

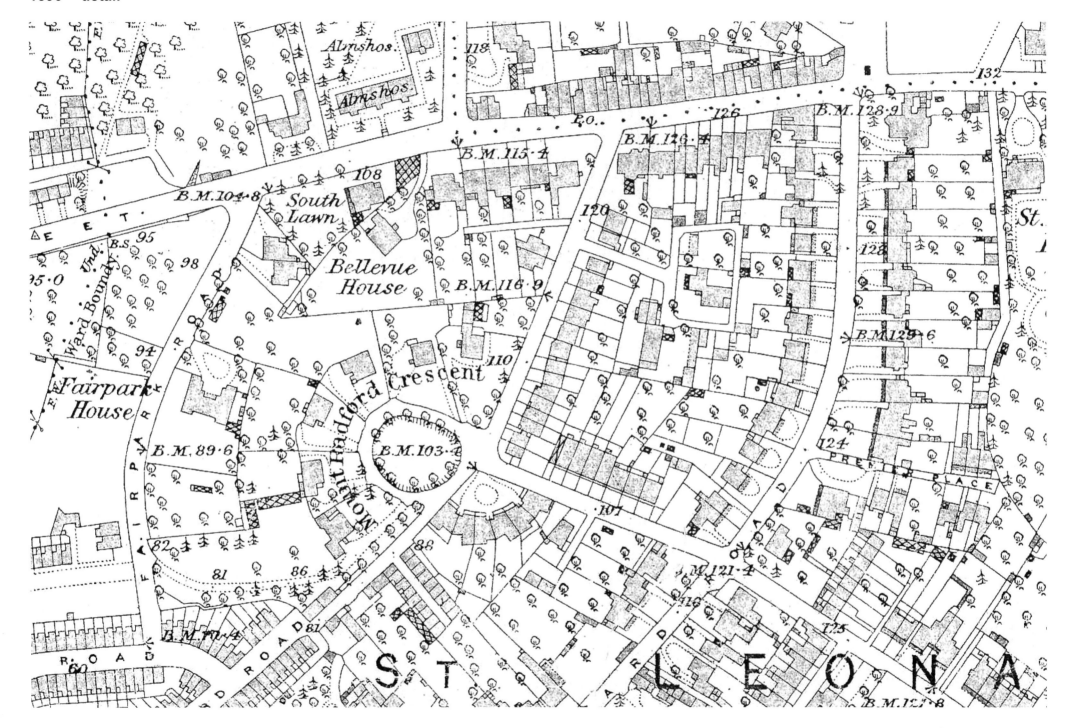

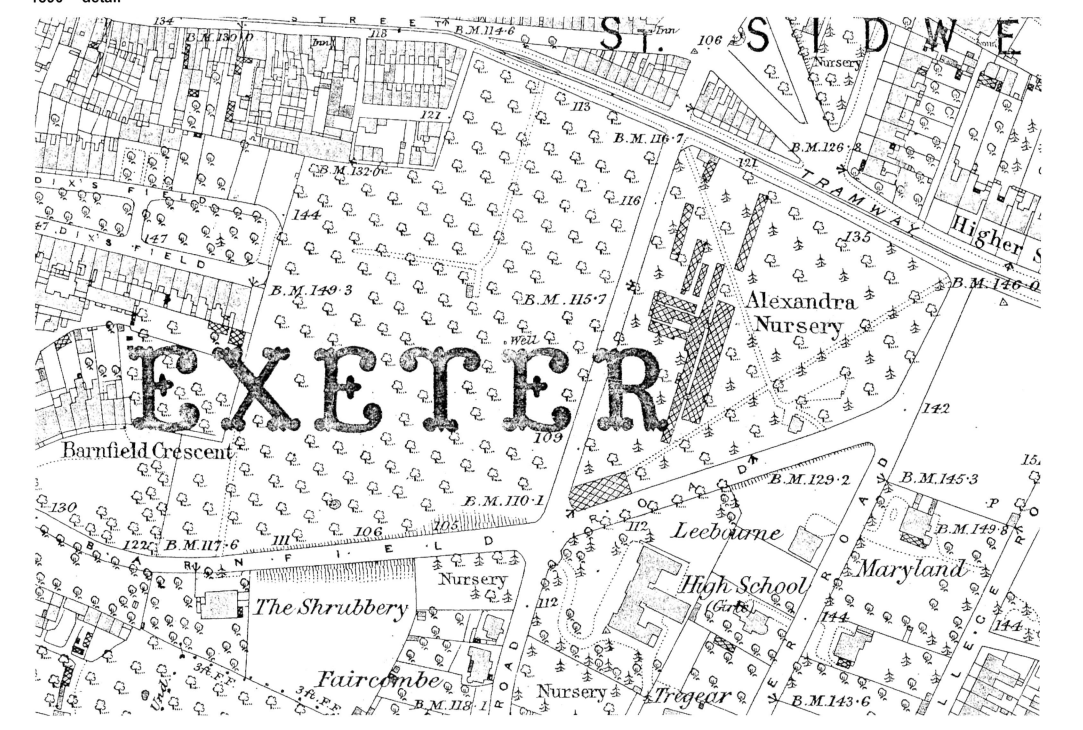

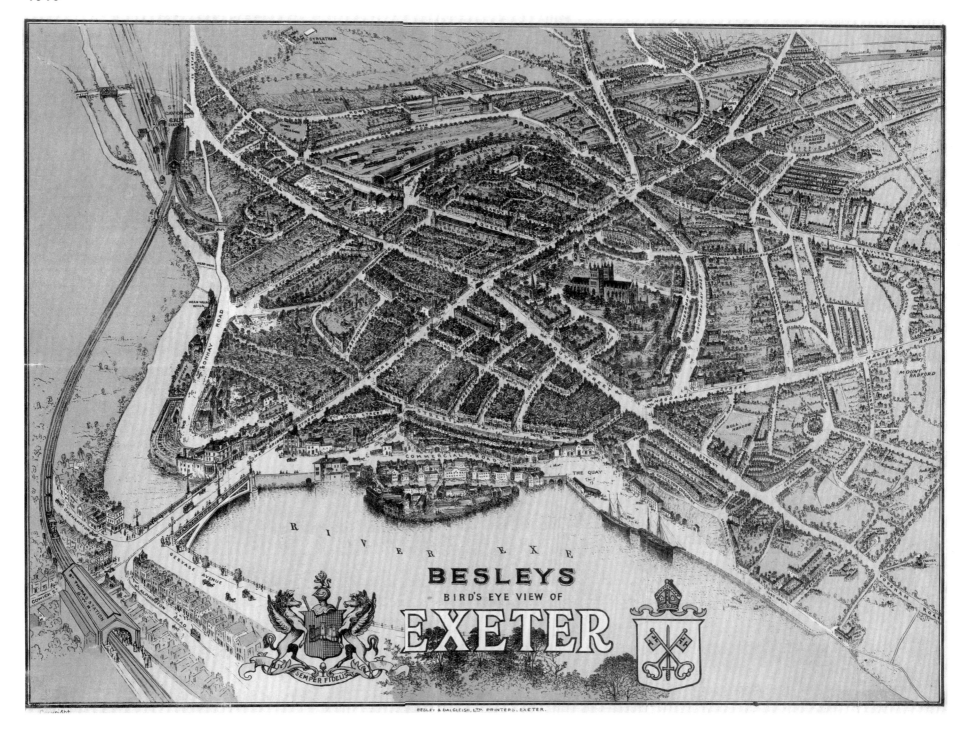

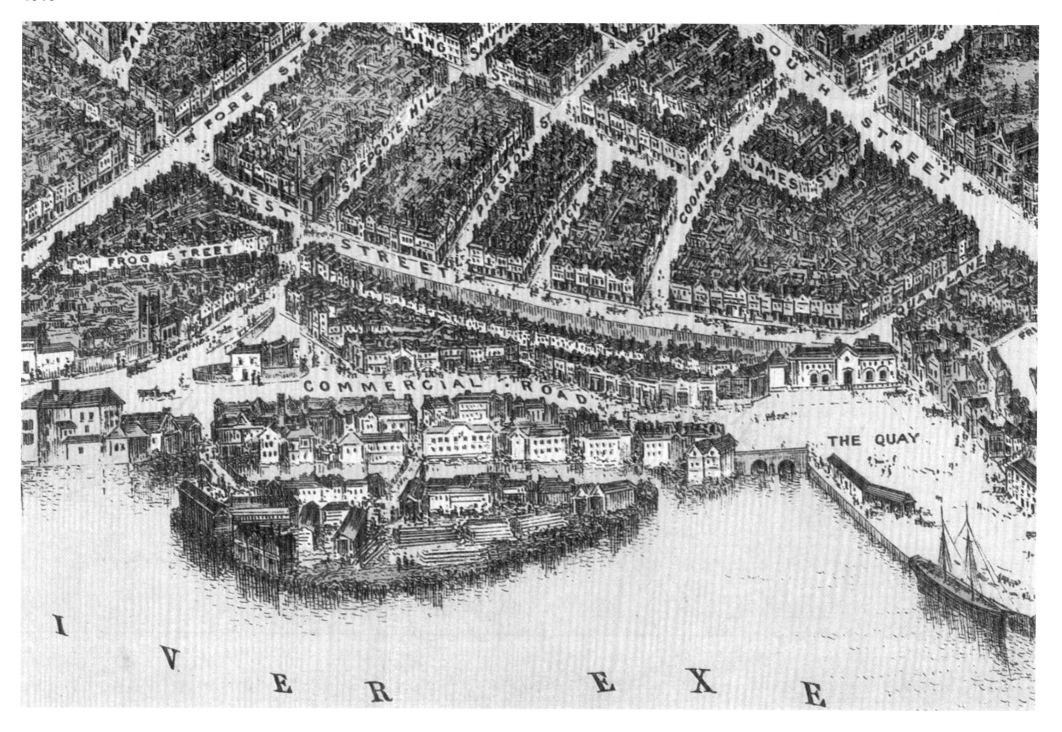

1941

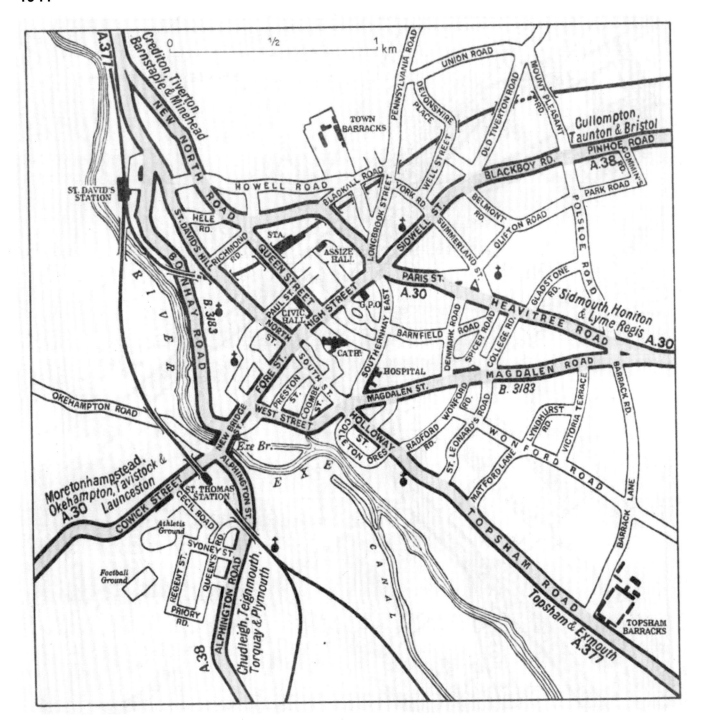